D0235771

Learning Resources Centre
Wallace High School
Airthrey Road
Stirling FK9 5HW
Telephone: 01786 462166

Return on or before the last date stamped below.

16 Nov 18			

Amazing Mysteries
GONE MISSING

John Townsend

W
FRANKLIN WATTS
LONDON·SYDNEY

An Appleseed Editions book

First published in 2009 by Franklin Watts

Franklin Watts
338 Euston Road, London NW1 3BH

Franklin Watts Australia
Level 17/207 Kent St, Sydney, NSW 2000

© 2009 Appleseed Editions

Appleseed Editions Ltd
Well House, Friars Hill, Guestling, East Sussex TN35 4ET

Created by Q2AMedia
Art Director: Rahul Dhiman
Designers: Harleen Mehta, Shilpi Sarkar
Picture Researcher: Amit Tigga
Line Artist: Sibi N. Devasia
Colouring Artist: Mahender Kumar

All rights reserved. No part of this publication may be reproduced, stored in a
retrieval system or transmitted in any form or by any means, electronic, mechanical,
photocopying, recording or otherwise, without prior permission of the publisher.

ISBN 978 0 7496 8800 4

Dewey classification: 001.9

WALLACE HIGH SCHOOL
LEARNING RESOURCES CENTRE
TEL: 01786 462166

All words in **bold** can be found in Glossary on pages 30–31.

Website information is correct at time of going to press. However, the publishers cannot
accept liability for any information or links found on third-party websites.

A CIP catalogue for this book is available from the British Library.

Picture credits
t=top b=bottom c=centre l=left r=right
Cover Image: Q2AMedia, Inset: Q2AMedia

Digital Vision/ Photolibrary: 4, Thomas Jackson/ Getty Images: 5b, Larry St. Pierre/ Shutterstock: 9r, Jeremy Walker/
Getty Images: 13r, Billy Black: 15t, Nara Archive: 16, Gelpi/ Shutterstock: 17, Redemption/ iStockphoto: 18c, Stephen Mallon/
Getty Images: 19b, Nicholas Rjabow/ Shutterstock: 20t, Digital Vision/ Photolibrary: 21, Thomas Barrat/ Shutterstock: 23b,
Douglas Miller/ Stringer/ Hulton Archive/ Getty Images: 24b, Sculpies/ Shutterstock: 25r, Angela Deane-Drummond/ Stringer/
Hulton Archive/ Getty Images: 27, James Carl Wise/ Contributor/ Getty Images, 28b, David Gowans: 29t.
Q2A Media Art Bank: Title Page, 6, 7, 8, 10, 11, 12, 14, 22, 26, 31.

Printed in China

Franklin Watts is a division of Hachette Children's Books,
an Hachette Livre UK company.
www.hachettelivre.co.uk

Contents

Where have they gone?

People go missing all the time. They just seem to vanish. Although many soon turn up again and others are found after a long time, some people will never be seen again. They vanish from the face of the Earth forever.

Answers?

Do people who disappear run away to start a new life? Perhaps they're unwell, need help or just forget who they are. Were they taken? Kidnappers, murderers or even **aliens** may snatch them away. Did they get lost, go the wrong way, fall or get stuck somewhere?

Can you believe it?

A **legend** tells of James Worson, a shoemaker who lived in Leamington Spa, England. In 1873, he bet friends he could run non-stop for 14 km to Coventry. He started to run, followed by some people in horse-drawn wagons who watched to make sure James didn't cheat. During the run, he stumbled and fell, "with a terrible cry". People watching said James vanished before he hit the ground. He was never seen again. Nobody could ever explain what happened.

! Some people disappear and are never seen or heard of again.

A famous case

Farmer David Lang and his two children, George and Sarah, were playing in the front yard. David decided to walk across a field to see his horses. A family friend, Judge August Peck, came by and David turned to walk back to the house, waving to the judge. A few seconds later, David Lang – in full view of his wife, his children and the judge – disappeared in mid-step.

Missing File

Date: 1880

Place: Tennessee, USA

Who: David Lang

Witnesses: Family and friend

Where did he go?

Everyone rushed to where David had been walking. They thought that he must have fallen into a hole or bog. But there was nothing there. A search by the family, friends and neighbours revealed nothing. A few months after the disappearance, the Lang children noticed that the grass on the spot where their father vanished had turned yellow in a circle about five metres across.

! Some people vanish into thin air in front of witnesses.

5

Missing at sea

There are many stories about ships and people that disappear forever at sea. No one knows where they have gone or can explain why they have vanished.

The *Mary Celeste*

The famous mystery of the deserted ship the *Mary Celeste* has never been solved. The ship set sail from New York in 1872, bound for Genoa in Italy.

Missing File

Date: 1872

Place: Atlantic Ocean, off Portugal

Who: Ten people on board *Mary Celeste*.

Witness: None

Empty ship

On board were its American captain, Benjamin Briggs, his wife and their two-year-old daughter, as well as a crew of seven men. A few days after leaving New York the *Mary Celeste* was seen drifting on the Atlantic Ocean near Portugal.

Discovery

Another American ship, the *Dei Gratia*, sailed close to the drifting *Mary Celeste*. Some of its crew climbed aboard and found the ship empty, its decks and sails wet and its lifeboat missing. There was no sign of a struggle on board the *Mary Celeste*, but all ten people who had been on the ship had vanished. They were never seen again.

! Captain Briggs, an experienced sailor, vanished with his family and crew.

Questions

Why would the captain and crew **abandon** ship? Nothing in the ship's log gave any clues. There was plenty of food and water on board. For years people have asked what happened. Did the lifeboat sink? Did they land on an island and die of thirst? Did a sea creature eat them all?

! We'll never know now what really happened on the *Mary Celeste*.

WHAT HAPPENED?

- ◎ Pirates? Nothing was stolen.
- ◎ Illness? Why would they ALL leave?
- ◎ Fighting? There was no blood or signs of violence.
- ◎ Bad weather? They'd be safer staying on board ship.
- ◎ Danger? Everything was safe and in order. The log book reported nothing unusual.

The *Ellen Austin*

Within 10 years of the *Mary Celeste* mystery, another ship's crew went missing. This mystery was not far from the island of Bermuda . . . in the area known as the Bermuda Triangle (see pages 14–17).

! The American **schooner** *Ellen Austin* often sailed from New York to London.

Missing File
Date: 1881
Place: Atlantic Ocean, off Bermuda
Who: Six sailors
Witness: No one saw what happened

ELLEN AUSTIN

Ghost ship

Captain Baker of the *Ellen Austin* saw a drifting ship with its sails flapping and masts swaying. He sent some of his crew to row over and take a look. As they climbed aboard the silent ship, the six men listened for signs of life. The lifeboats were still on the creaking, empty deck. No one was on board and nothing was out of place. There was no sign of any trouble. It was like a ghost ship. Captain Baker told his six sailors to stay on board and sail the mystery ship to the nearest port. A man called Morgan took charge.

Sailing to land

The two ships set sail together, expecting to reach land in a few days. As night fell, thick mist drifted around them. Captain Baker lost sight of the other ship as they sailed on through the dense fog. When daylight came, the fog slowly lifted. Captain Baker looked out across the water but there was just empty ocean as far as the eye could see. The **ghost ship** had disappeared.

Never solved

The story, with all its mystery and legend, became yet another of the sea's dark secrets . . . and the **fate** of the men missing in the mist has never been discovered. One story told of the mystery ship reappearing without Morgan and his crew on board. But who knows what really happened that night?

! The ghost ship was never seen again – nor were the captain and crew.

MYSTERY MOMENT

There are no lists for missing crew or casualties from the *Ellen Austin* among ships' records from the 1880s. Surely someone would have reported the names of the missing men placed on board a **derelict** ship which later disappeared?

The *Marlborough*

Another famous ship that disappeared was called the *Marlborough*. The mystery began when the ship set sail for London from New Zealand on 11 January, 1890 with 21 people on board. Two days later the *Marlborough* was seen by a passing vessel. From that time onwards, the ship was never heard of again.

No news

The *Marlborough* and its crew and captain never arrived in London. After many months had passed, the ship was declared 'missing', presumed sunk by icebergs near Cape Horn, at the southern end of South America. This is an area known for its fierce storms and freezing weather. Everyone on board was declared dead.

Missing File

Date: 1890

Place: Off South America

Who: 21 people – captain and crew

Witness: None – at first

! The *Marlborough* went missing in one century, and was not found until the next!

Discovery

The loss of the *Marlborough* was almost forgotten until 23 years later. In 1913, the crew of another ship sailing near **Cape Horn** spotted a drifter, which is a **vessel** that seems to be drifting aimlessly. A search party set off to climb aboard the drifter. No one was prepared for what they were about to find . . .

! Only skeletons were found on the *Marlborough* when the ship was rediscovered, 23 years after it first went missing.

EYE WITNESS

"At last we came up alongside her creaking hull. There was no sign of life on board. The mate and a number of the crew decided to board her. The sight that met their gaze was unbelievable. Below the wheel lay the skeleton of a man. Treading warily on the rotting decks, which cracked and broke in places as they walked, they encountered three more skeletons."

Unexplained

One skeleton was alone on the bridge. It may have been the captain. The remains of other bodies were found elsewhere. There was a spooky stillness all around on the ship and a smell of mould. In the captain's cabin were rotting books and a rusty sword. But the big question remained unanswered: what killed them? How had the ship remained unseen for 23 years? And why had it not smashed itself to pieces on the rocks of the South Atlantic coast?

The Flannan Isles lighthouse

The rocky isles in the Outer Hebrides to the north-west of Scotland still hold a mysterious secret. On Eilean Mor, the biggest island, is a lighthouse. It was there, in 1900, that three men vanished without trace.

Danger

The Eilean Mor lighthouse still flashes its light across the stormy seas to warn ships of the treacherous rocks. But today the light is automatic and no one needs to live in this remote place to keep the lamp working. But just over 100 years ago, three lighthouse keepers lived and worked there. The rocks were said to be haunted by dead sailors who perished in shipwrecks beneath the waves.

! No one lives in the Eilean Mor lighthouse today.

Missing File

Date: 1900

Place: Eilean Mor, Scottish island

Who: Three lighthouse keepers

Witness: None

Missing

On the day after Christmas, a small boat called at the lighthouse, as it did every two weeks. It brought food and picked up one of the lighthouse keepers to take him ashore. But for the first time ever, there was no one to greet the boat. Something was wrong. The lighthouse and the island were deathly quiet. There was no flag flying and no empty boxes to collect on the **jetty**. The landing party entered the deserted lighthouse.

Mystery

The main room in the lighthouse was clean and tidy. Food was in the cupboards and everything was just as it should have been. There were no oilskins hanging up, which was strange because all three men would never go outside at the same time. In the log book two weeks before was written, "*12th December. Waves very high. Tearing at lighthouse. Storm still raging, cannot go out.*" The very last entry was three days later at 1 pm on 15 December, "*Storm ended, sea calm. God is over all.*" That was the last ever entry written by the lighthouse keepers who were never seen again.

! Inside the lighthouse the clock had stopped, the fire was out and the three men who should have been on duty were nowhere to be seen.

WHAT HAPPENED?

◎ Some people say the missing men had been turned into crows by an ancient curse. Others said skeleton pirates might have carried them away. Or did aliens carry off the men? After all, **UFOs** have been reported in this part of the world. Or were all three men washed away by a freak wave? We will never know now.

The Bermuda Triangle

One area of the sea is more feared than any other. It is called the Bermuda Triangle. Aeroplanes and ships have entered this region between Florida, the Bahamas and Cuba . . . never to be seen again.

Sea of secrets

Some sailors say the Bermuda Triangle is just a **myth**. They blame bad sailors for getting lost and not knowing about the sea's strange currents. It is a busy shipping area, so there are bound to be a few losses sometimes. But other people think differently. Why have planes gone missing here? And why is wreckage hardly ever found? There are still many unanswered questions about this sea of secrets.

The USS *Cyclops*

The ship USS *Cyclops* was a large cargo ship, designed to carry coal. In 1919, the *Cyclops* sailed from the USA to Brazil to refuel British ships in the south Atlantic. It set off again from Brazil, stopped briefly in Barbados and then headed off through the Bermuda Triangle. The huge ship was never seen or heard from again. All 306 passengers and crew were gone without a trace.

! Each point of the
Bermuda Triangle is
about 1,600 km apart.

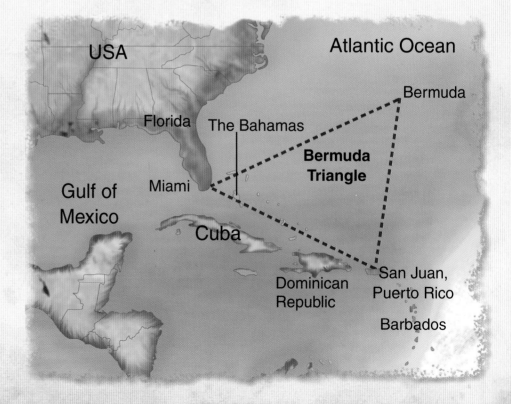

USA

Atlantic Ocean

Bermuda

Florida

The Bahamas

Bermuda
Triangle

Gulf of
Mexico

Miami

Cuba

Dominican
Republic

San Juan,
Puerto Rico

Barbados

! After Michael Plant set sail on his boat *Coyote* he was never seen again.

Missing File

Date: 1991

Place: Bermuda Triangle

Who: Michael Plant

Witness: None

Lost

In 1991, Michael Plant set off in his ocean racer, *Coyote*. Near Bermuda, he reported something strange. He kept losing electrical power and his radio began going wrong. Then all radio contact was lost and no more was heard. Months later his boat was found upside-down miles away. Michael was never found. He was yet another mystery from this strange ocean.

MYSTERY MOMENT

Perhaps time gets lost in the Bermuda Triangle. One story tells of a passenger plane disappearing from **radar** screens and the air traffic controllers feared the worst. But the Boeing 727 suddenly appeared again and landed safely 10 minutes later. The crew said they'd flown through fog and when they landed, all their clocks were 10 minutes slow!

Flight 19

One of the most famous disappearances in the Bermuda Triangle was Flight 19. The story of 27 men and six planes that vanished forever has puzzled the world for years. Where they all went and why was a big mystery at the end of 1945 and it still remains a secret.

Planes in trouble

On 5 December 1945, five Avenger **torpedo** bombers took off from the Fort Lauderdale Naval Air Station in Florida on a training flight over the sea. Charles Taylor was the officer in charge of 13 student airmen. He was in radio contact with all his fellow pilots. Over an hour into the flight, Taylor said his compass wasn't working and he wasn't sure where he was. The weather grew worse. It was hard to see and the pilots knew they were lost. Taylor said they should fly east but the planes were running out of fuel and it was getting dark.

> ### Missing File
> Date: 1945
> Place: Bermuda Triangle
> Who: 27 men
> Witness: None

! Five planes flew into the dark skies above the Bermuda Triangle . . . never to return.

No trace

The last signal from Flight 19 back to the air base was at 7.04 pm. After that the radios went dead. Rescue planes took off to search the area all night and through the next day. There was no sign anywhere of the five planes. Within hours of their disappearance, one of the search planes also went missing. It gave no distress signal but just vanished. There were 13 men on board, and they were never seen again.

Still searching

Ever since 1945, people have tried to find the remains of Flight 19. In 1991, five crashed aeroplanes were found in deep water off the coast of Florida. But divers found the engine numbers and proved that these were not the planes from Flight 19. The final resting place of the planes and crews of Flight 19 remains one of the Bermuda Triangle's dark secrets.

WHAT HAPPENED?

◎ Flight 19 is just one of the Bermuda Triangle mysteries. There were many other training accidents here between 1942 and 1945 during World War II. Including Flight 19, 94 air crew were 'lost' in total in this area. In many of the disappearances, no one really knows what happened.

❗ What secrets still hide in this mysterious ocean?

Vanished in America

Some people think that disappearances in the Bermuda Triangle, and elsewhere, may be something to do with UFOs. Do aliens kidnap humans so that they can study them? Many strange stories about people vanishing have been blamed on 'creatures from beyond'.

Missing File

Date: 1959

Place: Jacksonville, USA

Who: Bruce Campbell

Witness: None

❗ Could aliens have kidnapped Bruce Campbell?

The man who didn't come back

In 1959, Bruce Campbell was in bed beside his wife, Mabelita, when he disappeared. She was asleep and maybe he was, too. The Campbells were staying overnight in a hotel in Jacksonville, Illinois in the USA. Fifty-seven-year-old Bruce had driven all the way from their home in Massachusetts to visit their son and new grandson. He was very tired and was ready for bed.

Gone in his sleep?

Twice in the night Bruce woke to ask his wife if he'd locked the car. She told him not to worry and to go back to sleep. When she woke later at 2.15 am, she was alone and the space in the bed next to her was empty. A quick search found nothing apart from Bruce's wallet, money, shoes, glasses, keys and all his clothes. The only things missing were the green pyjamas he had worn to bed.

No clues

Despite police searches over many weeks and a reward for anyone who could find Bruce Campbell, he was never found. No one spotted a man 1.9 metres tall wearing green pyjamas, who walked with a limp. It seems he just vanished from the face of the Earth.

WHAT HAPPENED?

◎ Did he run away to start a new life? There have never been any sightings or reports of him.

◎ Did he go sleepwalking and fall down a hole somewhere? A body has never been found.

◎ Did someone or something kidnap him? There was never a **ransom note**.

◎ Was he **abducted** by aliens?

! Did Bruce Campbell sleepwalk into nowhere?

The DC-3 passenger plane was not **pressurised** like modern aircraft.

The strange case of Jerrold Potter

Some people really do seem to vanish into thin air. Jerrold Potter did just that – high up in the sky. In 1968, a small passenger plane took off from Kankakee, Illinois, to Dallas, Texas, USA. It was a clear summer's day and everything on board the flight was fine. Jerrold Potter told his wife Carrie that he was just going to the back of the plane to use the toilet. She never saw him again.

Where did he go?

After a while, Carrie grew concerned that Jerrold had been out of his seat for so long. She asked the staff to check if he was all right. But when they looked, the toilet was empty. In fact, he was nowhere on the plane. The DC-3 plane had a rear door that was just open. This didn't suck out the air from the plane, as it would in modern aircraft. A chain for keeping the door shut was found on the floor. Had Jerrold fallen out or jumped?

Missing File
Date: 1968
Place: Mid-air over the USA
Who: Jerrold Potter
Witness: None

Heavy door

Surely Jerrold Potter didn't fall against the door and fall out? For one thing, the door had a warning in large letters 'Do not open in flight.' But also, it had a heavy handle that had to be turned a full circle to release two huge bolts. No one saw or heard Jerrold fall. Some passengers later said the plane shuddered slightly a few minutes after Jerrold had walked past them. It was like a bump, as if the plane went through an air pocket. But even if this had thrown Jerrold against the door, surely people would have heard him or felt a gust of wind.

WHAT HAPPENED?
- If he fell, would he push the door almost shut behind him?
- Did he make a mistake and think the exit was the toilet door – despite the notice?
- Was he pushed by another passenger?
- Did he jump on purpose without a parachute?
- Was he ill or confused? His wife said NO.

No reason

Jerrold Potter was a 54-year-old businessman who was happy at work and at home. He was in a good mood at the time he disappeared and in good health. There was no reason why he should suddenly throw himself from a plane. So what DID happen to Jerrold Potter? A long search was made along the plane's flight path over the Ozark Mountains of Missouri. His body was never found and the mystery remains to this day.

! Did Jerrold Potter fall or was he pushed?

Driving into oblivion

Edward and Stephania Andrews were both 62 years old in 1970 when they vanished in their car. They were last seen leaving a cocktail party at the Chicago Sheraton Hotel in Illinois, USA. The couple were both in business and lived in a fine home in the Chicago suburb of Arlington Heights.

Seemed normal

Other people at the party said they behaved normally and seemed fine. But when they collected their car the parking attendant thought Stephania was crying and Edward didn't look well. As he drove away, Edward scraped the car on the exit, but he carried on going – heading north along the southbound lane! The attendant was the last person ever to see the Andrews again.

Mr Edward Andrews

Mrs Stephania Andrews

! Pictures of the missing couple were printed in the newspapers but no one knew where they were.

Missing File

Date: 1970

Place: Illinois, USA

Who: Edward and Stephania Andrews

Witness: None

They didn't reach home

The following Monday police were called to the Andrews' house when the couple were reported missing. Neither of them had appeared for work and letters had piled up in their mailbox. Inside their house, everything was tidy and the only items missing were the dress and jewellery Stephania Andrews had worn to the party.

Long investigation

Why the Andrews never arrived home, and where they went, has puzzled the police ever since. The case remains open and the police still ask for any information about the strange disappearance that night in Chicago.

WHAT HAPPENED?

◎ Maybe Edward had driven away, feeling ill and plunged off a bridge into the Chicago River. But a careful search found no sign of such an accident. The river was even dragged to find the wrecked car but nothing was found. The Andrews and their car had simply disappeared into the night and their file remains unsolved.

! There was no sign of either the Andrews or their car in Chicago's river.

Whatever happened to Lord Lucan?

A mystery gripped the UK in 1974. A well-known 40-year-old man named **Lord** Lucan, disappeared. There had been a murder at his home and it looked as if he may have been the killer.

Unhappy home

Lord Lucan lived in a smart London house with his wife and three children. Sandra Rivett was the children's nanny. But it wasn't a happy house. There were serious money problems and rows, and the marriage was all but over. Lord Lucan spent most of his time gambling at his club. But on a tragic night in November, the lives of this unhappy family hit the news. Newspapers were full of a murder story.

WOMAN FOUND DEAD

8th November, 1974

The body of a 29-year-old nanny has been found in the basement of the Lucan's home in London. Lady Lucan discovered the body last night. She ran out into the street shouting 'Murder!' Police are trying to trace Lord Lucan. It seems the nanny's killer had waited in the dark basement, ready to strike. When the nanny came in to switch on the light, a lump of pipe cracked down on her skull. Her killer bundled her into a sack. There was blood all over the room.

! A happy Lord Lucan on his wedding day.

Escape

Lady Lucan told the police how her husband had run into her bedroom covered in blood looking shocked. Then he started hitting her. She ran from the house and raised the alarm. By the time help came, Lord Lucan had fled. The police began a hunt for Lucan straight away but he was nowhere to be found.

! Who had been waiting in the dark that night?

MYSTERY MOMENT

The nanny was due to be out that night. But she changed her mind at the last moment. Did Lucan lay in wait to kill his wife … and kill the wrong woman by mistake? The nanny was the same size as his wife. Who could tell them apart in the dark? The police believe Lucan did it. Why else did he run from the murder scene, never to be seen again?

Manhunt

The police searched for Lord Lucan up and down the country. They knew his car was missing, so they assumed he had driven to an airport to leave England in a hurry. After a while, the police found Lucan's blood-stained car in Newhaven on the south coast. It was thought he must have run on to a ferry and escaped across the English Channel to France.

WHAT HAPPENED?

◎ Did Lord Lucan escape on a ferry? Did he get away in a speedboat? Maybe one of his friends helped him to hide. Many who knew him said he could never leave his children or live in another country. Some said that he must have killed himself. But his body has never been found.

Sightings

Seven months after Lord Lucan disappeared, a jury announced that he was guilty of murder. He became the 'most wanted' man in Europe. Or had he gone to South America or Australia to start a new life? Every few days people around the world reported seeing men who looked just like Lord Lucan.

❗ The police discovered Lord Lucan's abandoned car – with blood inside it.

Is Lucan alive?

Even in the 21st century reports appear in newspapers that Lord Lucan has been seen. One headline read: IS LORD LUCAN ALIVE IN AUSTRALIA? Someone was sure they had met him in Perth, Western Australia.

The mystery continues

Lord Lucan was officially declared dead in 1999. In October 2004, Scotland Yard re-opened the investigation into the murder. Detectives wanted to look again at all the evidence and to use modern **DNA profiling** to try to solve the case. Perhaps Lord Lucan had been a victim? Was he killed, too? We may find out one day.

! 20 May 1975: police take to the air to search for the missing Lord Lucan.

MYSTERY MOMENT

Just before he disappeared, Lord Lucan spoke to his friend, Susan Maxwell-Davis. He told her that he had tried to stop an **intruder** at his house who tried to kill his wife. This 'witness' believed Lord Lucan to be innocent.

The search continues

The search for missing people continues for many years. One such search in 2008 was for Steve Fossett, who disappeared over the Nevada Desert, USA, in 2007.

Adventure seeker

Steve Fossett was an American millionaire **adventurer**. He was famous for breaking all sorts of world records, including being the first person to fly solo non-stop around the world in a balloon in 2005 and 2006. In 2007, he took off in a small plane, but this time he never returned.

Missing File

Date: 2007

Place: Nevada, USA

Who: Steve Fossett

Witness: None

! Steve Fossett was famous for his exciting record-breaking travels.

Mystery

Steve Fossett went missing on 3 September 2007, after taking off in a small aircraft from a private Nevada airstrip. All contact with him was lost and he never returned. There were rumours that he may have faked his own death but in 2008, the courts declared that he was **legally dead**. Then in September that year, a hiker in the Sierra Nevada mountains found Steve Fossett's ID cards. A search of the area found the scattered wreckage of a burnt-out, crashed plane.

Who next?

Strange cases of missing people still baffle the experts. Such mysteries have puzzled the world for years. We're left with questions, to wonder where people have gone and if they will ever be found. In the time that it's taken you to look at this book, someone else will have been reported as 'gone missing'.

! Steve Fossett soared into the sky in a plane like this. . . never to be seen again.

WHAT HAPPENED?

◎ There is now no doubt that Steve Fossett's plane crashed soon after take-off. He probably died on impact. Search teams recovered two large human bones near the crash site. DNA tests confirmed that they were Steve Fossett's. The searchers thought that his body had been found and eaten by wild animals. But why did such an experienced flyer crash? That is still a mystery.

Glossary

abandon ship	an order given to the crew to leave a ship when it is in danger of sinking
abducted	to be taken away against your will
adventurer	someone who goes on dangerous and often exciting missions
alien	someone from another country — or planet
Cape Horn	a rocky headland at the southernmost tip of South America where the seas are stormy and dangerous
DNA profiling	testing the special code in each person's genes to identify patterns or types. This testing is used to discover more about evidence, such as blood or hair, which may be found at a crime scene
derelict	left abandoned by the owner or occupants
fate	the end result or final outcome
ghost ship	a mysterious ship that seems to be steered by ghostly sailors
intruder	someone who forces entry into a building without permission
jetty	a small landing pier for boats
legally dead	declared as 'deceased' (or dead) by law so that all paperwork can be completed
legend	a story from the past whose truth is often accepted but cannot be proved
Lord	a British peer who is entitled to sit in the House of Lords

myth	a popular belief that is passed on but which is usually false or unsupported
pressurised	kept at a normal air pressure. Modern aircraft are pressurised so that passengers can breathe comfortably at high altitude
radar	device for detecting and locating an object by the reflection of radio waves
ransom note	a written demand from a kidnapper, usually for a payment that must be made before a captured person is released
torpedo	a long narrow bomb, often fired through water
schooner	a fast sailing ship with at least two masts and with sails
UFO	the abbreviation for unidentified flying object
vessel	a hollow container, often describing a boat, ship or water craft

Index

Webfinder

http://morticom.com/categoryweirdearthdisappearances.htm
Read about some of the strange disappearances of people through history

http://bermuda-triangle.org/
Stories about missing people and craft in the Bermuda Triangle

http://www.castleofspirits.com/strangediss.html
Stories from around the world about people who have apparently vanished in thin air

http://www.lordlucan.com/
All about the Lord Lucan mystery